PREFACE

This is a REALLY short book.

It's really more of an *introduction* to the Repossible series, the Repossible ideas and philosophies.

In movie terms, this is like the *trailer*. It's short, it's sweet, it's going to highlight what's to come. But it's not the movie itself.

In fact, I hope that, just like a movie trailer, you decide to "watch the movie" or in this case, read the books but if not, I hope this book either saves you from heading down the path of an 11-book series or it lets you dip your toe in the water, you like how it feels, and you want to slowly slip all the way into the warm waters of Repossible.

The Radio Dial

I substituted for a teacher in a biology class for kids in high school, maybe 13-years old.

Quickly after I entered the room, I had the distinct feeling that many of the students didn't want to be there. In fact, I'm pretty sure they would have rather been ANYWHERE else other than in a biology class with a substitute teacher.

In fact, we started talking about exactly that and not biology—why are we places we don't want to be?

They loved the question and also loved telling me how much they didn't want to be there. It was OK with me, I didn't want to be there either—at least, not as a biology teacher.

But when we got onto the other topic, the one about What They Really Wanted, then they opened up and we connected.

I see it like an old-fashioned radio dial. The kind where you had to turn it just right to get the station the most clearly.

It was like that with the kids. We weren't even on the right frequency until I tuned into them and we were as clear as glass.

If you read this short book and feel like you don't want to be here, please don't stick around on my account.

Although I would ask this. Where might we connect? What are you missing that you see in Repossible?

Where might I change the dial and then find the frequency where you and I can talk to each other?

Enjoy Repossible and if you don't, no harm done, class dismissed, and you have a hall pass to go somewhere you enjoy and truly where you want to be.

CONTENTS

REPOSSIBLE

WHO WILL YOU BE NEXT?

BRADLEY CHARBONNEAU

REPOSSIBLE

PRAISE FOR EVERY SINGLE DAY

A QUICK SELECTION OF BOOK REVIEWS FROM PEOPLE WHO
ARE NOT MY MOM

If you're new to my ~~work~~ play, you might like to have a quick read of what other books of mine have done to help transform the lives of readers just like you.

I especially like how "P.C." writes below "There's a **spark** within me that has been relit."

I get my inspiration and content from you and I hope to keep up that connection.

Here are a selection of reviews for "Every Single Day."

~

"Somehow, I found myself devouring this today. It's rare that I allow myself this indulgence as the list of what I need to be doing in my head is endless.

Deliciousness to my soul, is the description that comes to mind as I reflect on my experience of consuming this book. I have no idea how to write a review and put into words **how deeply this resonated within me.**

There's a spark within me that has been relit. I know **ESD is the kindling I need to get the fire crackling and roaring** ... there are flames here that need to breathe and light the world.

Thank you Bradley Charbonneau for accepting the challenge of ESD, so that today, you could influence my ESD."

— 5 STARS FROM P.C. VIA AMAZON

~

"I love how you handle **deep subjects in such a light-hearted way.**"

— K<small>AY</small> B<small>OLDEN</small>

~

"**Before reading this book I was ashamed of myself.**

For years I had called myself an artist but I knew the truth. I was only masquerading as one. ... But could I continue to call myself an artist when I stoped making artwork? The answers is no.

I am not entirely sure what happened to me from the time I was in college until now, eight years later. There was **a shift that took place** in my mind during that time.

I **developed a fear** of making artwork. I would always make excuses as to why I just couldn't create. I was too tired, the dog needed a bath, I needed to do dishes. What was the point of painting anyway **because no one would want to buy or look at my work** etc.

I have spent many years working dead end jobs just to pay bills. I **never even allowed myself a chance** at having a career because I would give up at the slightest failure or rejection.

The few times I did really try, I won awards at competitions.

I now have a two-year-old son. I have used him as an **excuse** to not make art for the past two years. I **feel guilty** that I put so much blame on my son. Taking care of him was just a convenient excuse that is easily believed by most people.

After reading this book, there is no going back. I have no choice.

I make artwork everyday and I am happy. ... I know there is no going back.

I was miserable with guilt and now I am not.

I was afraid to create and now I happy to learn once more.

When I started to draw again I was really rusty but I got through it. I find time even though I take care of my son all day and I babysit my nephew for eight and a half hours a day.

I wrote this review in the hope that I could inspire someone else to change their life.

Take the Every Single Day challenge. Read this book it just might change your life."

— Paige

~

"The author shows us how to get past "analysis paralysis" to actually start projects and see them through until completion.

A theme of this book is to dream about doing something until the dream itself is internalized along with the willingness to progress toward goal completion in iterative steps taken each day. Readers will learn the importance of getting past inertia in order to begin complex tasks and progress toward a completion date with certainty.

Everyone who moves toward a meritorious goal must first start, stumble, reassess and move ahead with a refined approach toward reaching the goals set forth at the outset. Very few, if any, tasks are completed with zero failure points or stumbles. A strong point of the book is that the author sets up readers for roadblocks which must be overcome as part of the learning process. The book could be labelled alternatively as "what it takes to succeed"!"

— Dr. Joseph S. Maresca, Amazon "Hall of Fame" Reviewer

~

"He lights a path that you can choose to walk down."

— RAY SIMON, ACCOMPLISHED SPEAKER, AND A NO-LONGER-
SECRET TRUMPET PLAYER

"Never mind searching for who you are. Search for the person you aspire to be."

— ROBERT BRAULT

DEDICATION

For Saskia

INTRODUCTION
REPOSSIBLE

66 "It always seems impossible until it's done."

— NELSON MANDELA

It was so clear.

Sitting on the steps of Union Square having a Chipotle burrito with John Muldoon.

"If you don't buy it in the next five seconds, I'm going to buy it," he threatened.

He said it nice but I knew he meant what he said.

I bought it.

Over the next few years, we talked about it but didn't take much action.

We dreamed and even dared but didn't do much.

We discussed and might have even dabbled in a bit of design but didn't get too far.

But it wasn't going away.

Lots of ideas come and go.

Most go.

This one wasn't going anywhere.

Until I took action.

Until I did something about it.

Otherwise, it would haunt me until I did.

The purchase went through and I just bought a name we couldn't believe was available as an exact dot com.

Repossible.com

It was so clear then.

It was often clear along the way.

It is so clear now.

It's Repossible.

1. Repossible
2. Every Single Day
3. Ask
4. Dare
5. Create
6. Decide
7. Meditate
8. Spark
9. Surrender
10. Play
11. Celebrate
12. Evaluate
13. Elevate
14. Share

Each one is just a little verb. Some of them seemingly so innocent. Others might take months out of your life. Still others might gift you years you never knew you had.

Before we dive in, say each verb aloud and see which ones resonate with you.

Because you and these verbs are about to become very, very good friends.

FOREWORD

BY SOMEONE ELSE

" "If I am through learning, I am through."

— John Wooden

I don't have a foreword yet—at least not in the traditional sense that someone else writes it.

At this moment, there are 14 books in the series. I could see it going on until I run out of verbs.

But as Coach Wooden says above, when I am through learning, I am through.

I'd ask him to write the foreword but he's no longer with us—at least he no longer has a physical seat on the court.

When I was 12-years old, I went down the steps in Pauley Pavilion to ask him to sign his book, "Practical Modern Basketball." He did. I still have it.

If I am through learning, I am through.

I feel like I'm just getting started.

Here we go.

1

REPOSSIBLE

WHO WILL YOU BE NEXT?

> "The difference between the impossible and the possible lies in a man's determination."
>
> — TOMMY LASORDA

Before 2012, I had come to the conclusion that the life I had dreamt of living just wouldn't happen.

I was sad about it but I thought, "I guess that's just the way it is."

Well, *sad* is a tiny little word.

Let me start off this book real.

I was depressed, without hope or energy, full of regret, anger, and yes, sadness.

I had imagined my life as being something that I was so far from I couldn't see it happening anytime soon and probably not ever.

I was doing work I hated in a city I no longer loved and I was empty of desire and full of despair.

You know those moments in the movies, usually accompanied by dramatic music, when lightning strikes or the guy hangs on to the cliff by his pinky toe and then miraculously saves himself (and probably the rest of the planet) and goes on to cure cancer and star in the remake of The Shawshank Redemption?

Yeah, well, it didn't happen like that for me.

For me, it was walking down Larkin Street in San Francisco on the way to a dumpy Burmese place when I "came out of the closet" to one of my closest friends and said I wanted to be a writer.

But that I wasn't.

I had given up.

- The stars aren't aligned.
- The universe must not really have my back.
- It's a conspiracy!

I didn't yet know about the big verbs.

I didn't know how to Ask, I didn't Dare Decide to Create. I wouldn't have known how to Meditate if it Sparked me in the face. The only thing I Surrendered to was my sad fate. Play was for those kids on the swings and the closest I got to Elevate was in the elevator.

Then I changed my habit. Just one. I say "I" did it but I had help. John Muldoon coerced me into writing Every Single Day.

Not the book, but the concept of daily writing.

The verbs came.

The ideas blossomed.

Repossible grew from a seed of nothing into a tree of something.

I can barely remember that guy on Larkin Street, crying my tears of woe.

But he got me here so I thank him.

But between that guy and the person I am today is what you have in your hands.

What you have in your hands is Repossible.

- **Possible**
- **Impossible**
- **Repossible**

Oh, by the way.

This is me reaching out my hand to you.

Here we go.

I'm rooting for you.

2

EVERY SINGLE DAY

DAILY HABITS TO CREATE UNSTOPPABLE SUCCESS, ACHIEVE
GOALS FASTER, AND UNLEASH YOUR EXTRAORDINARY
POTENTIAL

"You need, more than anything else, daily momentum. It's the secret of all life happiness."

— BRENDON BURCHARD

"Only brush the teeth you want to keep," the dentist recommended.

"Uh, I want to keep all of them," I mumbled.

"Oh good, then you know exactly what to do–and how often."

I brush all of my teeth every single day.

Because I want to keep them (all of them) and if I just do it a few minutes every single day then I can not only keep them, but keep them healthy, strong, and help to prevent disease and cavities.

When we're talking about our lives, the kind of people we are, our challenges, dreams, and desires, it's as simple as brushing our teeth.

Which days do you want to be the person you've always dreamt of becoming?

If your answer is not every single day then you can put down this book right now and forget the entire Repossible series. Save yourself 11 (or more...) books, videos, courses, in-person conferences and whatever else may come from the Repossible and Every Single Day movements.

If "Every Other Thursday" is about your level of passion towards your life then, well, lucky you and you're free now to move about the cabin.

If, on the other hand, you're curious about personal development and you're looking to change or improve yourself or maybe just scoop up a little more joy in your life, read on.

Every Single Day is the extremely complicated scheduling methodology I devised after a couple of decades of going more along the lines of the Every Other Thursday strategy.

That's a little joke, nothing I do is extremely complicated...I
don't even know how to do something complicated.

On November 1, 2012, my life took a turn I would never return to. It was a point of no return when I decided to dare to create.

Catch that?

I love dropping hints about what's to come.

But before we decide or dare or even create, we need to ask.

The first question is simple:

Are you ready?

P.S. Disclaimer: My answer is often "Uh, no." Then I go ahead and do it anyway.

- **Possible:** tomorrow
- **Impossible:** yesterday
- **Repossible:** Every Single Day

3

ASK

RAISE YOUR HAND, EMPOWER KNOWLEDGE, AND LEAPFROG
YOUR OWN SELF.

"Whatever we are waiting for—peace of mind, contentment, grace, the inner awareness of simple abundance—it will surely come to us, but only when we are ready to receive it with an open and grateful heart."

— SARAH BAN BREATHNACH

Three little letters. Ugh. Wow. Dam.

Readers ask which book of the Repossible series is the "best" or which was the "hardest to write."

I'm a pretty laid-back kind of guy. I take the slow train. I'm patient.

I don't like the idea of making "the hard book the first book" but I don't see a way around it.

I thought Create could be first, or maybe Decide but Ask was like that festering wound that won't go away until you get it treated or worse, that piece of popcorn kernel stuck in your teeth the ENTIRE movie and all you can think about is removing it.

Yes, Ask is painful like that.

Annoying, little, and it won't go away until you address it.

Ask.

You have to ask the question.

"What am I supposed to ask?"

I hear you. That's yet another difficult part of this. Later on, we'll talk about asking for help and even daring to ask for help from others but first it's going to get even nastier, dirtier, and more painful.

Yeah, I know. Sorry about that.

You need to ask yourself.

Stuff like, oh, I don't know, let's toss around some questions:

- Who am I?
- What is my purpose in life?
- Why was I placed on the planet?

OK, too much too soon?

Let's take it down a notch.

- What can I do today to make tomorrow better?
- How can I be stronger so I become stronger to help those around me?
- If I do A, what are the chances of B actually happening and the risk of C happening first?

Feeling better?

Remember me? I'm that light-hearted guy. I'll prove it.

- Should I put "Oud Amsterdam" or parmesan on my popcorn?
- Should we do nothing this weekend or truly absolutely nothing?
- Is this pizza still fresh enough to eat?

So many questions. Maybe not so many answers.

But we have to ask the questions–we have to ask the question.

It's hard. It can be no fun at all. It's easier to just avoid it.

> "Can't we just skip to an easier topic? Something more lively like Spark or Play?"

See what happened there? A question was asked. It always starts with a question.

Here, I'll give you an easy one:

Are you ready?

- **Possible:** avoid
- **Impossible:** answer
- **Repossible:** ask

4

DARE

DO SOMETHING DIFFERENT, THEN DEVELOP FOR, DISCUSS
WITH, AND DISTRIBUTE TO DOMINATE THOSE WHO DIDN'T
DARE DO.

"Far better is it to dare mighty things, to win glorious triumphs, even though checkered by failure... than to rank with those poor spirits who neither enjoy nor suffer much, because they live in a gray twilight that knows not victory nor defeat."

— THEODORE ROOSEVELT

Remember back in Ask how I said it was too bad to start off with something difficult?

I wish I could say Dare was easier.

It might be even harder.

Asking is often out of our comfort zone. It takes practice, we can get better, we can also learn to ask better questions and we often get better answers.

We're not even to the point of Deciding what to do with those answers or Creating based on what we know we need to do.

Nope. Sorry.

We're at the point where we Dare do what we previously might have never done.

Let me call on someone from the audience to show an example. Anyone? You in the blue shirt? No? OK, fine, me.

1. **Ask:** I asked myself what kind of person I wanted to be.
2. **Dare:** I had the audacity to dare to dream big and be the author I had always thought I would be.

It's a bit like an answer.
I dared to do.
Then I did.
Now I don't dare not do.
Now that we dared to get out of our comfort zone, it's time to Create.

- **Possible:** don't
- **Impossible:** dodge
- **Repossible:** dare

5
___

CREATE

STEP AWAY FROM THE SCREEN, SPILL YOUR SECRET POWER,
AND UNLOCK YOUR LIFE.

> "When it is obvious that the goals cannot be reached,
> don't adjust the goals, adjust the action steps."

— CONFUCIUS

I wish this were book #1. In fact, don't tell anyone but you could make this #1 if you think it fits.

I "really" started writing on November 1, 2012, when John Muldoon "forced" me into a 30-day challenge to write every day--just for those 30 days!

I'm probably going to get in trouble for saying this for each one of the Repossible series but if you had to only pick one book, this one would be it.

Without creating every day, writing every single day, I would be nowhere. Well, not nowhere, I'd probably still be at Ask.

I'm going to get brutal here. Hold onto your hats.

I don't care how many degrees you have, how often you meditate, who you know, how you got to where you are, or how fantastic the rest of the world thinks you are, you need to let it out.

You need to create.

You need to make, do, act, build, write, paint, draw, express, let it go, let it out, and get over it.

Then do more.

Then some more.

Tired yet?

Awesome.

Do it some more.

I don't give in on this point. Without creating, I don't know who we are. Or let me rephrase, I wouldn't know who I am.

How can we know who we are if we don't express it? Exhaust, exhale.

You know the simple and easy bit? Some things are simple but not easy and vice-versa. I know you know it.

Creating is simple and easy.

Sorry, you might say it's hard.

> "I have writer's block! I don't know what to say/write/do/paint/sing."
>
> — You

I might believe that you don't "know" but that still not excuse enough.

Just do.

Just write.

Just sing.

You have fingers? You can find a pen? Maybe a napkin, a paper, your palm?

You can write. You can do, make, build. If I haven't hammered this home enough, you might just need to read the book.

I have one power. I am consistent. I am persistent. I am patient, powerful, and I do one thing every single day.

Create.

- **Possible:** consume
- **Impossible:** contain
- **Repossible:** create

DECIDE

THERE'S USUALLY A CHOICE. IT'S USUALLY YOURS.

> "Take a chance! All life is a chance. The man who goes farthest is generally the one who is willing to do and dare."
>
> — DALE CARNEGIE

Death and taxes.

There, I got the things out of the way where you don't have a choice.

Are we done here?

In the Repossible series, we dig into some fairly meaty topics: purpose in life, meaning on the planet, joy, happiness, etc.

I could also dig deep right here and now and say we need to make The Big Decisions and choose at the fork in the road to become the person we have always dreamed of being or stick to the same path of the one we've accidentally become.

But hey, we're still in this Repossible book so I'm going to give you a bit of fun.

Decision making is a skill. It's a muscle. We can get better at it and the muscle can get stronger.

A colleague of mine at the naming agency where I worked couldn't make a choice on a restaurant menu to save her life--or eat. It frustrated me to no end.

> "Just get the salad."
> "Can you make up your mind already?"
> "I don't care anymore, I'm going to bathroom. I hope you've made a decision by the time I'm back."
>
> — ME

It was just *lunch*.

We can learn to use our gut, our heart, and our minds to shoot for a "best two out of three" vote and make better decisions faster.

We can then make decisions such as:

> "Will I finish this book?"
> "Will I do the exercises?"
> "Should I stop eating potato chips every night?"
>
> — YOU

Then we can grow and learn and improve so then, yes, we're going there, we can get to the hard stuff:

> "Will I ever become the person I hoped to have become?"
> "When will I take the first step towards my freedom?" (HINT: now is good)
> "How can I come out of hiding and unleash my true self to the world?"
>
> — YOU

Those last three may sound daunting but once you can order lunch, you're on your way to deciding just about anything.

No, really.

I finally decided to become a writer. The book in your hands is my 19th book.

It took small decisions and then some big ones. Some really big ones. ("Should we move to Europe?" "Should I close down my marketing agency?" "Should I become the writer I know I truly am?")

Yep, I answered those.

You might decide to join me and waltz along the Repossible Trail. You might decide to get lunch.

You might just get the salad.

I'm rooting for you.

- **Possible:** delay
- **Impossible:** dither
- **Repossible:** decide

MEDITATE
WHEN YOU'RE READY TO TAKE YOUR SUCCESS TO THE NEXT
LEVEL.

"You should sit in meditation for 20 minutes a day, unless you're too busy. Then you should sit for an hour."

— Dr. Sukhraj Dhillon (probably)

I do my best to live a life without regrets. Not too many, "Oh, I wish I had only..." But I do have a big one.

I wish I had started earlier with meditation.

I don't say this lightly as not only do I try to not carry regrets but when I do have them, I'm not happy about them.

I can hear the meditating elite saying to me:

"Just meditate to relieve yourself of those regrets."

— Some guru in Nepal

The thing is, they'd be right.

The thing is, I don't have a more powerful book in the Repossible Series than Meditate.

I'm going to get in big trouble for saying this because I'm already catching myself saying it for a few of the books but I can't not say it here.

> "If there's one book that's the most powerful, the one you can't let slip by, that single book you'd shove into the hands of both your dearest friend as well as your fiercest enemy, it's Meditate."
>
> — IDEALLY SOME LOVELY REVIEWER

I couldn't have written this book in 2012 when I started writing, when I turned my life around (and my life turned around on me, when I started to Create).

Probably, no, almost certainly, had I known about the power of meditation previously, I wouldn't have had to suffer through not becoming the person I wanted to become.

Who knows, had I found meditation earlier, this book wouldn't be in your hands because I probably wouldn't have had this escapade, this treacherous path, my years-long journey through the slog and pain of getting to where I am today.

Maybe meditation only works--or works best--if there's something to heal, to fix, to, well, meditate on. Maybe if your life is perfect and you don't need any help or guidance or anything or anyone, maybe meditation is just like watching a movie: kinda fun just without the popcorn.

I don't know. That didn't happen to me.

I slogged through the years of fighting with myself. I battled, cried, pouted, screamed, and fought my way to get where I am today.

Then I found meditation.

Then I took things up a level. To quote from upcoming titles in the Repossible Series, I Surrendered, I was introduced to the enlightenment of Play.

I can't emphasize this one enough. If I had to give up all books and have only one, just one thing or "skill" or talent or idea I could continue on with, it would be Meditate (or Create).

But Meditate elevates Creation.

Now I'm getting ahead of myself.

I can't describe it. Yet I have to write a book about it.

Maybe I need to Create in order to figure out what Meditate means to me.

Please, if not for your own sake, then for mine, for those around you, for those younger than you who will grow up in your wake, who will feel the frequency of your being, take Meditate with you and give it a chance.

- **Possible:** pretend
- **Impossible:** reject
- **Repossible:** meditate

8

SPARK

WRITE A SHORT BOOK WITH YOUR KIDS, IGNITE THEIR
CREATIVITY, AND CHANGE YOUR RELATIONSHIP FOREVER

> "With patience and persistence, even the smallest act of
> discipleship or the tiniest ember of belief can become a
> blazing bonfire of a consecrated life. In fact, that's how
> most bonfires begin—as a simple spark."
>
> — DIETER F. UCHTDORF

As we rocket upwards and onwards with our own selves, we're going to take what might seem like a detour but is actually more of rocket fuel.

Spark sneaks into the <u>Repossible lineup</u> to cooperate, coordinate, and collaborate.

For seven books, we've been focusing on ourselves, our greater selves, and everything in between.

We'll get back to "us" but this book takes us beyond the "us" of you and me and reaches out a hand to someone we're going to lift up.

Spark began after years of people asking me to put together some sort of guidelines or workshop or at least a book to help them do what my kids did: write a short book.

> "I sat on the red chair in the living room with my 8-year-old son having just read a not-all-that-great children's book. "We could do better than that," he said. Three weeks later we had a book on Amazon."

— ME

What came out of that time wasn't just a book but an experience, a relationship, an adventure between father and sons (my other son, then 10 joined us). We went on to write four more books together and recently I teamed up with my 17-year-old nieces to write two more books.

The emotions and power we felt are almost too much for words. But hey, I'm an author, I can find the words. I'm going to go bullet points on you here because they are flowing out of me faster than I can put into sentences.

1. Pride
2. Purpose
3. Meaning
4. Joy
5. Tears
6. Accomplishment
7. Chance
8. Hope
9. Trust
10. Power

That list of 10 took me all of 10 seconds.

Spark has become a workshop where we write a short book (or create "something from nothing") or song or film or _____ and we do it together. That's it.

I don't have many rules but one is of utmost importance:

Get It Done.

I go on and on about mathematics but there are only two numbers you really need to understand: 0 and 1.

0 is zero is nothing is before you get started.

1 is one is that first step and it's all you need to get to the finish line.

You keep adding 1 to another 1 and soon you have several and you have a book or a song or a film and when the month is up or your just feel it (whichever comes first), you're done.

I'm also a stickler for Getting It Done because, and this might sound a little odd if this is your first book we'll be doing together, but I want this first book to be your *worst* book ever.

Why? Because we'll improve with each book.

Do you know what you can't improve on? I'm going back to math here. You can't improve on nothing.

Do you know what you can do with nothing?

Nothing.

Which is where the Spark comes in. We spark the creativity in another human (usually someone younger, maybe related to you) to get them going, to lead them along, to be their guiding light.

We have a (private) Facebook group of moms, dads, uncles, and rockstars who have now written books with their kids, created films with them, and formed relationships and bonds that will withstand the tests of time.

If I'm asked in which of the Repossible books my heart lies, it's Spark.

You'll see, all of this personal development is great and all but when you can help someone else, when you extend your reach to another human and lift them up, even if just to get up from the floor, you'll feel a bolt of lightning strike and a rumble of thunder will rattle your heart like nothing you could have ever done on your own.

That's Spark. It's my love. It's my baby. I'm sharing it with you.

- **Possible:** create
- **Impossible:** hide
- **Repossible:** spark

9

SURRENDER
GIVE UP, GIVE IN, GIVE BACK, AND GET MORE THAN YOU EVER IMAGINED.

> "If you knew who walked beside you at all times, on the path that you have chosen, you could never experience fear or doubt again."
>
> — WAYNE DYER

Here we are at book number nine in the Repossible series. If I can't yet be honest and open and spill my true guts to you by now then I don't know when I ever could.

With "Every Single Day," I told you my story of how I battled, slogged through the mud of years of doubt and denial, and finally made some progress by sticking to a simple daily regimen of creating.

Had I stopped there, I would have been good.

The thing is, I wasn't (and still am not) really looking for "good." Sure, I was looking for better than it was and I certainly got that.

The thing about success and happiness and joy and meaning and purpose in life is that they're...addictive.

You want more.

The good news?

There's plenty more where that came from.

The bad news?

You have to surrender.

I like the dictionary and thesaurus. But there's so much about "giving up" and "losing" to the enemy and all that. Still, although I thought about other verbs (give in, release, let go, allow), they just don't have the power of surrender.

If you read book seven (<u>Meditate</u>) then you'll know I'm ready for more, I'm always seeking and searching and finding and discovering. I'm rising and falling, learning and churning.

But I'm having a good time doing it.

Can we go back to the quote up top?

> "If you knew who walked beside you at all times, on the path that you have chosen, you could never experience fear or doubt again."
>
> — WAYNE DYER

I don't care who you think the "who" is beside you. If it's God or a god or a fairy with wings or another religious figure or a beam of light or a candy cane. Or if it's a higher version of your own self. Or an angel. Or your father. Or mother. Or uncle Rudy.

To get past book number nine here, we're going to have to give in that there is some greater force beyond our brains, deeper than our hearts, and more intuitive than our guts.

I hear you, I hear you. "Uh oh, Bradley has gone off the deep end."

If my deep end involves letting go of my personal limits and allowing the unknown of the universe to come in and guide me then yes, I have gone off the deep end.

I'm both trying to tread lightly here because I want to bring you along (because I want to show you the glorious gardens beyond the wall) and also daring to venture beyond where you're comfortable and might abandon me.

The thing about the "might abandon me" part is that I believe it's more along the lines of "might abandon you."

If I've gone too airy-fairy for you, let me reel you back into reality with this. My morning meditation, my surrender to a higher power that I do every morning, is the source of my power, is the energy behind this multiple-book series, is the beat of my heart and the idea to do a program to bring kids and parents together through writing a book.

It's where my Big Ideas come from. It's when I Know What To Do. It's how I Get Stuff Done.

It's my time machine. I can spend 17 minutes in meditation, surrender to the unknown, and be ahead on my day by eight in the morning.

It's my secret weapon--yet it's no longer secret because I'm telling you about it right now.

It's also not mine. That's why I dare write this book. It's mine, it's yours, it's ours.

Join me in daring to create a level higher than you ever imagined. Spark a new light in your self that illuminates something you have always dreamed of but never thought would come to fruition.

Surrender to that higher power. Don't be scared. It's just you. It's the you of your dreams, it's the self of your imagination, it's the good, pure, powerful body that walks beside you at all times and silently has your hand and lifts you up towards a world that is yours.

- **Possible:** give up
- **Impossible:** fight
- **Repossible:** surrender

10

PLAY

GET OFF THE BENCH, OUT OF YOUR MIND, AND INTO
THE GAME

> "Work consists of whatever a body is obliged to do. Play
> consists of whatever a body is not obliged to do."
>
> — MARK TWAIN

I couldn't have written this book back in 2012 when I began to Write Every Day. Sure, I knew the word Play but it was more in the sense of a game, usually with a basketball or maybe dice.

Frankly, back on November 1, 2012, I couldn't have written any of the books in the Repossible series. I was at a point of desperation, of overwhelm, of cloudy and muddy thoughts about the future.

I could only function, I could barely get words onto a page, I was surviving, dreaming of thriving but happy to get by.

So the concept of play back then was untouchable, unreachable, impossible.

I begin with this as I don't take the concept of play lightly.

Ha, that's a joke.

Lightly is exactly how I now approach it.

In fact, lightly is the only way you're going to get anywhere near the mindset, the philosophy, the elevated level of play.

The Repossible Series isn't in a strict order but a few of the concepts do usually need to come before the others. For most of us mere mortals, Play needs to come after Surrender.

To accept the idea that Play is OK, that's it's acceptable, and, hold onto your hats, that it's the desired level of our life's regular status, takes some daring, some decision making, and some surrendering.

I fully realize that I am making excuses for this enchanted level of awareness but that's only to appease the me of the past, that guy who would have heard of the idea of Play and scoffed and gotten back to work.

But that was then. That was him.

This is now. This is you.

If you're this far, if you want to elevate to the level of Play, you're probably already here.

Let's see if I can define it or at least dance around the concept enough to entice you to waltz onto the stage and join us.

The easiest way to describe it is to go back in time. Way back. To you as a child when life was simple, had very few responsibilities and the drama in your life perhaps revolved around topics relating to toast, bicycle tires, and laughing.

At the Play level of Repossible, there is lots of laughing.

There are also smiles, winks, and inside jokes.

It's as if the world, as if our world, is a playground. A place where we frolic and even giggle.

Yes, I said it. Giggle.

Listen here, tough-guy reader. I dare you, I challenge you, I double-dare you to giggle.

You can do it on your own. You can quickly get over it in the car on the highway or maybe it's better to wait until you're parked.

It's a sly laugh. It's a knowing smile. It's a feeling, an awareness of a higher level of self.

I saw a bumper sticker once that said something like:

"If you're not in awe you're not paying attention."

— Bumper Sticker

There's a childlike wonder. A deep curiosity. A state of mind you have--or have had--so you know it's there but you may no longer believe it's real.

Sort of like Santa Claus.

I'm not here to say that Santa Claus is real.

I'm here to say that Play is real.

It's up to you to find it.

Here, take my hand. I know the way.

- **Possible:** work
- **Impossible:** neither work or play
- **Repossible:** play

11

CELEBRATE

HONOR YESTERDAY, REJOICE TODAY, AND SURPRISE
TOMORROW

"Celebrate your successes. Find some humor in your failures."

— SAM WALTON

I was doing an apprenticeship in a large German firm. My German was pretty good and I was learning the language—and the business—pretty fast.

But the copy machine?

That thing was a mystery, a monster.

I'm pretty sure that machine could fold laundry, staple your paper lunch bag, and, oh yeah, make copies, too.

It was both my enemy and my guru.

I practically bowed down to its greatness when I had a "high-level" task such as *collate and staple*.

I must have hit 1.) staple and THEN 2.) collate because it was all mangled.

I laughed.

I laughed *at myself*.

A man who was later to become my boss there approached me and was wondering why I was laughing.

I explained.

He asked me if it was correct that I was laughing at my failure.

I suppose I hadn't thought quite about it like that but I confirmed that this is exactly what I was doing.

He did that thing people do when their eyebrows go up, their lips turn upwards into an upside-down half moon, and nod their head and say, "Hmmmmm."

Much later, *years* later, that man told me how impressed he was that I could laugh *at* myself, *especially* while I was making a mistake.

In a twisted way, I was *celebrating my failure*.

This book is about celebrating the little stuff. The seemingly insignificant stuff.

As wondrous as that story is about an experience I had in Germany, I'm writing this book because I don't celebrate the small wins often enough.

I'm much more guilty of:

1. Trying
2. Doing
3. Succeeding
4. Moving onto something new

I know, it's the cliché of stopping to smell the flowers. But remember how much truth there usually is in clichés!

The next book in the series, Evaluate, is going to "require" some celebration in order to move on.

In other words, we need to get the Celebrate verb into our user's manual, into our company rulebook, into our habits.

For example, you just finished a chapter.

Go ahead, pat yourself on the shoulder.

If anyone asked why you're congratulating yourself, you can just say, "I just finished a chapter."

Discuss why that's important when they give you that look. You know the one. With the raised eyebrows, the curled lip, and the "Hmmmmm."

- **Possible:** wait for the next bigger success
- **Impossible:** celebrate every single moment
- **Repossible:** celebrate every chance you get

12

EVALUATE
SO, HOW'S IT GOING?

> "If you can not measure it, you can not improve it."
>
> — WILLIAM THOMSON, LORD KELVIN

In searching for the quote for this chapter, I also came across the more famous version:

> "What gets measured gets managed."
>
> — PETER DRUCKER

Upon further research, you get the full quote.

> "What gets measured gets managed—even when it's pointless to measure and manage it, and even if it harms the purpose of the organization to do so."
>
> — PETER DRUCKER

This chapter, this book, is a tough one for me. It squarely lands in the category of:

> "Yes, Bradley, you need to write this book because you need it even more than your audience."
>
> — One of the Little Guys Sitting on my Shoulder

As of November 1, 2012, I wrote Every Single Day. I even kept a log (evaluate?) of each day here: Write Every Day.

By recording, keeping track, and logging my work, was that *evaluating* what I was doing?

Honestly? Not really.

I was just writing. I just kept going. I didn't look forward or back, I just did the work every single day.

If I now look back, yep, I improved my writing, I got in the writing habit, I have written 25+ books since that day I began.

So if I now evaluate and look back and ask, "OK, how did I do? How am I doing now? Where am I heading?" then I can see the progress.

Here's the thing.

If I had stopped after writing Every Single Day, I'd be good. Then I went on to work at Trader Joe's or the HEMA, I could have looked back, evaluated, and said, "Yep, that was a great success."

But I kept going.

I kept learning, improving, building, growing, discovering, exploring, playing, enjoying, collaborating.

I felt like I didn't have time to evaluate, I was too busy doing!

Isn't that book five? Create?

Isn't that good enough?

- Just create stuff, man!
- You're good!
- Keep going, you'll get there!

But *where* are you going?

What's next?

Why are you doing, creating, making, building? Doing the stuff you do?

How's it going?

Can you know where you're going next if you haven't evaluated where you came from? Where you are now?

This is where this is tough for me.

The thing is that I don't mind just creating. I love creating. Creating is my thing, it's my mojo, my modus operandi.

I can't not create.

I don't evaluate how my teeth brushing has gone!

I don't evaluate if I walk better in the woods!

Yet I'm doing fine with both of those things.

That's it: "I'm doing fine."

If that's good enough, we're done here.

I'm Doing Fine

I've been *doing fine* for years, decades even. Seriously. Really fine.

The next book is called Elevate. It's about taking all of this, all of these books, these steps on a ladder, up to the next level.

But here's how I see it: elevate is about taking the entire ladder up to the next floor.

You're in, I don't know, a shopping mall, and you take the whole ladder, your entire last few years of work or life, and get on the escalator and take it all up to the next level.

Yep, that's my plan.

Yep, that's my hope for you.

This is where evaluate comes in.

Where am I now?

Where did I come from?

What's up on that next level?

Here, super real life: for me, it's about going from being a writer to being a speaker.

I have spent the past 7 years working towards being a writer. You know how I'm doing?

I'm Doing Fine

I'm laughing to myself as I type this.

Yep, I'm doing fine. It's fine. Things are fine. I'm fine.

Yep.

What's next?

As much as I'm appreciating the moment, carpe diem, and living in the present, I'm addicted to growing, to learning. Does curiosity kill the cat?

I hope curiosity kills me. I can't think of a better way to go.

I'm curious about that next level up there at the shopping mall. I have my ladder on my shoulder and I'm ready to elevate.

But first, I need to evaluate. I need to acknowledge where I was, where I am now, celebrate, and assess where it is I want to go.

Sure, I could stay on this level for the rest of my life—just like I'm going to brush my teeth the rest of my life.

But this goes (hopefully!) a little deeper than teeth brushing.

This is your next life. Not afterlife (that's a whole other books series...). This life, this next life, your next chapter.

Because you thought this was good?

Just wait until you get on the escalator.

- **Possible:** plunge forward without a plan ahead or even a glance back to the past
- **Impossible:** only move forward when having evaluated the plan
- **Repossible:** evaluate

13

ELEVATE

ASCEND THE MOUNTAIN, ADMIRE THE VIEW, RELISH THE
ALPS IN THE DISTANCE

" "It's what you learn after you know it all that counts."

— JOHN WOODEN

It's now early 2020 as I write this. This book is scheduled for the spring of 2021. My own personal elevation is writing this Repossible book series.

Have I already achieved the "elevation" I'm going to be writing about?

Yes and no.

Yes because I'm writing this series. Yes because I'm living this series. Yes because I have passed the point of no return. I can't "go back down" to where I was before.

No because I'm always ascending, always learning, always on the lookout for a new peak to climb.

I'm an extremely visual person. I see many things in line graphs (yes, I was a dorky math major at some point). I also tend to see mountains.

Elevate might get you to the top of the mountain but what I'm more interested in is what you do when you get there.

You could choose to:

1. Celebrate and go back down from where you came,
2. Celebrate and ponder where to go next,
3. Celebrate and look out over the horizon and take the first step towards it,
4. Have a sandwich.

OK, you could combine #4 with one of the others but for me, and this is relatively recent, I'm mostly doing #3.

Don't take this the wrong way. Don't see this as the endless struggle, the road with no end, the life-long battle.

I hope I can shed a positive, even playful light on this.

We celebrate at the top and revel in the feeling that we know we will only go higher.

We pop the champagne, truly and deeply enjoy the moment, yet still smile quietly to ourselves because we know we have ascended but a single peak in an alpine region of behemoths.

We know how to Play. We know how to Meditate, to Create, to Spark others. We will no longer descend, we cannot, we don't even know how to go back from where we came.

We are now the ascended.

Oops, I just made us sound divine.

Wait a minute. Let me check.

Nope, that's OK.

We are the ascended.

We are up there, we choose what to do next, where to go, whom to bring with us.

What is even more fun than attaining this height is starting the path towards the next one.

It's a game, it's a joy, it's love.

We become, we are, we elevate.

- **Possible:** descend
- **Impossible:** stay

- **Repossible:** elevate

14

SHARE

TELL YOUR STORY, SPREAD YOUR SUCCESS, AND EMPOWER
OTHERS TO BEGIN

" "Success is best when it's shared."

— HOWARD SCHULTZ

H ere we are at the top of the mountain. Woo hoo! The view is great, we can see our next challenge in the distance, and it's possible that we're...alone.

My mom passed away recently. The other day I wanted to share a tiny little success story with her. In a weird way, my success is more real when I can share it.

There is a fine line between boastful bragging and sharing your success.

Hopefully, after you've achieved the levels of Spark and Play (and especially Surrender), you've come to realize that you didn't get here alone.

You've also hopefully come to believe that we're Better Together and a shared win is more powerful than a solo victory.

So whereas bragging might be seen as, "Ha, look what I did (and you're not there yet)!" or "You'll never get as far as I have!" using a sense of superiority and especially exclusion, the share model is deeply engrained in inclusivity, joint efforts, and the idea that a rising tide lifts all boats.

Happiness, joy, pride, purpose, meaning are not zero-sum games. In other words, if someone has some happiness it doesn't mean there is less left over for you.

In fact, dare I venture to be so bold to say that sharing your story of success is the opposite of a zero-sum game. By sharing your wins and inviting others to take their own first steps (or further steps), we are making the pot bigger, we are rising the entire tide so much that all boats, ours included, will be lifted.

Did you catch that bit?

By sharing your win, you lift them but you also *lift yourself even more.*

Sounds great, right? You win. They win. We all win together.

It's not just pride or confidence that is building within you but through the telling of your story, through pulling others up with you, we are elevating the entire playing field with all of the players but also the entire game.

I was at a writer's conference in London and someone gave an example of a nonfiction book helping **just one person.**

He explained it with an elaborate story about his sister being outside and she needed help. What if you, inside, could help her, solve her challenge, fix her problem?

Yet you might say, "Oh, but I'm not expert enough, I'm not a guru in that field, there are so many other people who could help her and do a better job of it."

"But she's right outside that door and could really use immediate help and you're right here right now. All you have to do is step out the door and talk with her, tell her your story."

Would we really have any reason to not do it? Could we really think up more excuses to not go help her?

We're here in book number fourteen of the Repossible series. If I may boast for a moment about you, you have made progress. I don't know how much and it doesn't really matter but if you're this far, chances are good that you've made progress.

Now think back to before you began.

Now think of the girl outside.

She needs your help. Even if it's just your story. Even if it's just you telling your tale of success in a way that she might think, "Hmm, maybe I could do it, too. If he did it, why can't I? He's a real person and he started out at the starting point, too, right where I am right now and yet he's here sharing his success with me."

Even the second grade kid can help the first grade kid. She's been there before, been through it, escaped out the other side and lived to tell about it.

You could start your talk with the girl outside as simply as this:

> *"I've been where you are, I took the first step, I made progress, and now I am continually succeeding."*

Or even more simply:

> *"I have done it and you can, too."*

Of course, as the author of the Repossible series, I have my favorite books. There are certain books that resonate with me more strongly than others.

But this book? Share?

I'm not going to let up on this one.

I know first hand the power of testimonials, reviews, and story telling to share a success.

I, Bradley Charbonneau, could blab on and on about the wonders of the Repossible System—and in fact, I have done just that for 14 books! :-)

But when (not if...) you, dear reader, share your story of how you went from Point A to Point B (or to Point See...) with someone else, it verifies it, it sets it in stone, and it makes it believable and *real*.

Real to the point where someone says:

> *"I can do that, too."*

That's the power of share.

- **Possible:** tell only yourself (over and over)
- **Impossible:** keep quiet
- **Repossible:** share

I'm going to make it all very real. I'm collecting success stories of Repossible at share.repossible.com.

ROADMAP TO REPOSSIBLE

ROADMAP.REPOSSIBLE.COM

> "Apparently there is nothing that cannot happen today."
>
> — Mark Twain

If you dig deep into the annals of domain name registration, you'll find that I bought repossible.com right around the time I started writing.

I didn't do much with the domain (or even the concept) for years but I knew it was something. I knew it was something *bigger than me.*

I don't see Repossible as mine but as ours. I don't want it to be "Bradley's Collection of Oddities and Super Natural Powers."

I want it to be OUR collection of oddities and super natural powers.

Our collection of our quirks and stories, our own paths and detours, our messages, our voices, our unique oddities—what makes us unique.

But "super natural powers"? Really?

Yes.

Really.

Because that's exactly what our powers are: super and natural. We all have them, it's just a question of dusting them off or digging them up or fine tuning that radio dial to connect to the frequency that matches up your naturally super power with the even greater powers of your super natural self.

What does Repossible mean to you at this moment? Maybe before you've read any of the books? What does each of the words below mean to you?

1. Repossible
2. Every Single Day
3. Ask
4. Dare
5. Create
6. Decide
7. Meditate
8. Spark
9. Surrender
10. Play
11. Celebrate
12. Evaluate
13. Elevate
14. Share

If this is something of a probably-not-very-linear Roadmap to Repossible, where are you along the way? No idea? Have a thought or two? Or maybe you know exactly where are you and where you're heading.

The Roadmap to Repossible

If you were driving cross country, unless you've already done it numerous times, you're probably going to need a map.

You hopefully know where you are right now. You might have some idea of where you're heading. But how are you going to get there? What do you want to experience along the way? What do you know you need to do? What would be the most fun to do? What are you scared of? What are you looking forward to?

1. **Repossible:** Are you right here at the starting point? The opening shot that sets you off on the Road to **Repossible**?

2. **Every Single Day:** Maybe you'd like to start by reading (or listening to) the journey of someone else who has traveled the whole route from depressed, confused, and hopeless wanna-be writer to playful, buoyant, and unstoppable creator who is writing these words right here? It's all there in gruesome and glorious detail in **Every Single Day**.

3. **Ask:** Or maybe you are **Asking** yourself what your future might be? If all of this hype even sounds remotely possible and if it is—could it be possible for you?

4. **Dare:** It could be that you've already asked the hard questions—and some of the easy ones—and it's time to **Dare** to answer them. All day I can ask, "Who will I be next?" and "Is this possible for me?" but until I Dare to answer those questions, I'm still just at the roadside stop after Asking.

5. **Create:** When you've Dared to at least take the first step, your next question might very well be, "Well, what do I actually do now? How do I take action if I'm going to Dare to answer my questions?" You could read more books, attend more workshops, or listen to more gurus suggest what you should do. But at this point, I believe it needs to come from within, from you, it needs to not be something you take in, that you consume, but something you need to **Create**.

6. **Decide:** Only when it comes from inside of you can you judge, weigh the pros and cons, get that feeling if it's the right path or not, and then you can **Decide** to continue in this direction or maybe head back to Ask and pose your

questions in another way or Dare to answer other
questions.

7. **Meditate:** You know how sometimes it's really annoying
   when people say, "Yeah, I just know. I don't know why but I
   just do." Even though you may have just Created a rational
   and logical Decision and you're ready to move forward, it's
   time to call in the jury. It's time to go beyond our natural,
   conscious selves and bring in the big guns: our super
   natural unconscious greater power. It's time to **Meditate.** If
   there's one scenic overlook I would have skipped as my old
   self, it would be the idea of Meditation. Yet as my new self,
   it's the one I would most strongly, most passionately and
   with the most conviction recommend at least giving an
   open mind to.

8. **Spark:** Although things are now probably cruising along
   for you and you and you and you, it might seem like a
   detour and it might seem early in the journey but it's time
   to **Spark** what you have experienced so far in someone
   else. You don't need to be an expert, a guru, or the best in
   the world to reach out your hand and help someone up
   who is behind you in this roadmap. All you need to be is
   one stop ahead of them and help them up. Sparking the
   electricity in others is one of the most rewarding stops
   along the Road to Repossible. We are Better Together.

9. **Surrender:** Way back when you Dared to take action, you
   leveled up to a point past where you had been before.
   Then you Meditated and connected with your higher self.
   Through Sparking the energy in another person, you have
   again elevated yourself to heights you may have previously
   not experienced. It's now time to cash in some of that
   experience, to believe in a power that is greater than
   yourself—yet in yourself—and it's time to **Surrender** to
   your intuition, your super natural power, and the Brand
   New U.

10. **Play:** Way back at the lower frequency stops around Ask

and Dare, it might have seemed like you were just stuck at
a dirty gas station on the highway with the bathrooms
you'd rather forget you ever visited. At that point, way
back then, you might not have been even able to imagine
the ease, the simplicity, and the beauty of what was ahead.
Having now Surrendered to your own greater power,
Sparked the gift of giving into another human being,
Created your path, and having now risen up to a level
where it's fun, even funny, and there is more joy in your
daily life, it's time to **Play**.

11. **Celebrate:** Pull off to the side of the road. Yes, even if it's
    just in the ditch. Turn off the engine. Turn around in your
    driver's seat and look back at where you came from. Even
    if you can still see the starting point, you have made
    progress. Maybe you're so far along now you can't even
    see, you can't even remember or understand where you
    started. Whether it's been 1 step forward or 1,000, it's
    almost always time to **Celebrate**.

12. **Evaluate:** Whether you have just popped the champagne
    (you might want to drive out of the ditch and get to where
    you're going to spend the night first...) or you're simply
    acknowledging your progress with a sly smile of joy and
    pride, this is often the best time to take measure of where
    you started, let in sink in deep that you are now where you
    have arrived, and believe in where you're going and that
    you'll get there. It's time to weigh, vote, learn, choose, and
    Evaluate. Keep going.

13. **Elevate:** You have arrived. The weird part is, when you get
    to Elevate, you'll know what I mean when I say, "I'm here
    but there is no way I'm stopping. I can't stop. I'm a fire-
    breathing, glorious goddess of joyful energy and although
    I have reached the mountaintop, in spite of the fact that I
    am where I wanted to go, from this new perspective, this
    perch atop the summit, I know I am going to take things to
    the next level with new Asking, new Daring, new Creating

and the car, the map, the road, it's all a level up, it's the next big journey and maybe it'll get started in 7 years or in 7 minutes but I'm an unstoppable fireball of love and I know there's only one thing left to do, bring it all with me forward and **Elevate**."

14. **Share:** Dare I say this is the most important element of all. You have ascended from Asking the hard questions to Daring to answer them. You have Created and Decided, Meditated and Surrendered. You have come so far, been through so much, and to keep this all to yourself would be an injustice to humanity. It is now your duty, dare I say, your calling to tell your story, spread your successes, and empower those not quite here yet to begin. You pick your daffodil of experience, success, and power and **Share**.

Yeah, so you've got that going for you, which is nice.

There you have it, the Roadmap to Repossible. If you'd like to take a Repossible assessment and see where you are or even might be along the path, come join us at the friendly roadside assistance center at roadmap.repossible.com.

- **Possible:** go it alone
- **Impossible:** take a plane and skip the scenic route
- **Repossible:** join us on the Roadmap to Repossible

BRAND NEW U.

"If a caterpillar, with its tiny brain and zero education and not a single weekend workshop, can transform who it is and go from a blob of walking goo to a magical, colorful, flying sparkle of undeniable beauty, then who is to say that we, as unlimited humans with natural and super powers, with intent and passion and both persistence and patience, not be able to slightly alter our paths to turn into someone who sees the world more clearly, can figure out his or her roadmap towards a glorious new destiny, and become an unstoppable, magnificent, and glorious Brand New You?"

— BRADLEY CHARBONNEAU

Toying with taglines.

I tend to use these books as my sandbox, a playground, my sketchbook for new ideas.

As Repossible is coming to life and I'm going to boost it with a shot of adrenaline in the early 2020's, what it means is coming to light.

I just returned from the world's largest author conference, 20Books® Vegas, where I saw a need for some nonfiction-specific marketing and branding help.

Upon my return home and

1. away from "writers" and
2. back to "creators" and
3. entrepreneurs but then also
4. transformers, I see it's more than just writing and authors and even nonfiction authors.

There's a term I quite like called:

Transformational Nonfiction

I write books that, I hope, transform people's lives. Whether it's a tiny daily habit or a closer relationship with someone or coming out of a creative closet and blossoming into their true selves, it's all Repossible, it's transformative, and it's more than just nonfiction.

Being the branding and creative guy that I am, I see it more than just books and courses and speaking–although that's the core of it.

But it's about personalities, branding, marketing, people, co-creating, working together, learning, teaching, and relationships.

There's so much more to it than "just writing books." Don't get me wrong, at my core, I'm a writer. I can't not write. I'll never be able to not write–nor would I want to. Why would I stop the activity that gives me joy, clarity, meaning, and pays the mortgage?

Yet, how can I build the brand? How can I reach more people?

- Brand New U.
- Brand New You

I'm a rabid fan of playing with words and letters and I just can't pass up an opportunity.

Brand & Brand

- Brand: branding, marketing
- Brand: brand-spanking new

New

New: fresh, transformed, changed

You & U.

- **You:** that person who you are–and that other one you've become
- **U.:** We're always learning, teaching, sharing, and in class

Brand New U.
I like it.
I'll see if it sticks around in my mind.

- **Possible:** think about this idea but don't take action
- **Impossible:** Try to find the admissions requirements office to the personal development program at the University of Branding for People Ready for a Change in Their Lives
- **Repossible:** Brand New U.

Head over to bnu.repossible.com to see how to renew your personal brand and make it you.

ABOUT THE AUTHOR

> "I was not naturally talented. I didn't sing, dance or act, though working around that minor detail made me inventive."
>
> — STEVE MARTIN

I know I keep comparing the individual books in this book. This one is good for that. The other one is best for this.

But without "Every Single Day," I'd be daydreaming at the base of a tree in the woods with nothing tangible to show for it.

We can ask, dare, and create but consistency, just a tiny bit every single day, builds from nothing into something.

Once you're good with building small things, the big things start to take shape.

When you can stand on top of those and see over the trees, it's time for the larger-than-life ideas.

This is Repossible.

This is my nineteenth book.

It is far, far, far from my last.

If you would like to begin a short journey Every Single Day writing habits, come join the party, for free, at playbook.repossible.com.

Find, ask, dare, create, and play at:
bradleycharbonneau.com

facebook.com/bradley.charbonneau.author
twitter.com/brathocha
instagram.com/brathocha

ALSO BY BRADLEY CHARBONNEAU

Most of my books are also available as audiobooks (which I giddily narrate). Search for my name at your favorite audiobook distributor, slip on your headphones, and let me take you away.

Repossible

1. Repossible
2. Every Single Day (+ Playbook)
3. Ask
4. Dare
5. Create
6. Decide
7. Meditate
8. Spark
9. Surrender
10. Play
11. Celebrate (2021)
12. Evaluate (2021)
13. Elevate (2021)
14. Share (2021)

Frequency

Every Single Day

Every Single Day Playbook

Every Single Day Kids

Every Single Day Teens (I want to write this one because I want to read this one...)

Every Single Day Parents

Charlie Holiday

Now Is Your Chance (1)

Second Chance (2)

Chance of a Lifetime (3)

For Creatives

Audio for Authors

Meditation for Creatives (2020)

Shorts

Secret Bus to Paradise

Where I (Already) Am

Pass the Sour Cream

A Trip to Hel

Drive-By Dropping

Li & Lu

The Secret of Kite Hill (1)

The Secret of Markree Castle (2)

The Key to Markree Castle (3)

The Gift of Markree Castle (4)

Driehoek (5)

Really Old ...

urban travel guide SAN FRANCISCO

THE END

This is the last page of this little book.

It's also the beginning of your foray into the world of Repossible.

Remember, I'm rooting for you.

www.ingramcontent.com/pod-product-compliance
Lightning Source LLC
Chambersburg PA
CBHW060659030426
42337CB00017B/2692